FIREFLY

LOST IN THE INFINITY OF TIME

ANUSTHA PAL

This book is dedicated to each every person who inspire me to write and let

me

do whatever i wanted.I really want to give a special thanks to parents for

becoming

my biggest support and encouraging me in this work. after that I want

thank to

Notion press for helping me to become a published author, and this made a

great

impact on my life and make me my better version.

Contents

Contents

Foreword

The author of this book is Ms Anustha Pal, started writing since she was 19.

she took her graduation is bachelor of technology in computer science,

this book is

is her 8th book and it was written after the end of graduation. This book

contain beautiful

Poems of unshared life experiences and what Poetess saw in her

sorroundings.

her previous books are Scars,Door to my soul,Anustha diary,

Aeipathy,Under my umbrella,

Flashbacks in my cassette,I m Poet and now this new book "Firefly".she

chooses this name

for this book cause she wants to lighten the lifes through her poetry.

Preface

This book is a beautiful collection of Poems which have different flavour and
feel.
these Poems is expression of life and facts of about life.In very short the
poetess
of this book is love to write soulful content, So most of the Poem are
Soulful genre.
there is alot of dreamy characters are present in this book that you can
enjoy.
I am sure all the readers enjoy reading this book .

1. Closet

***here the poetess is considering the life as a closet and telling the
story in her thoughts.***

i am closet,
lock from past few years,
i wish to hear,
but there is no sound near,
i have frozen voice,
no frequency and no vibration.
but just lost into never ending
darkness,
in my gates there are termites
they spoiling my insane,
i wish i have chronicles
of naria to see,
another world of other
dimension i am holding
in me,
i wish some one come,
to see my individuality,
to know what i may be
and warm my frozen voice
so that i can speak.

2. Hanky

in this poetess want to convey that sometimes we all are very much anxious
of several small things, and we can't able to deal with them and live that moments
with our tears and they are only comfort zone for us in that time.

hanky of this world is Small,
Can't wrap up my tears.
The silhouette of my home
Standing in back,
Can't handle my fears.
The fishes at my home,
live in the pond of my tears,
they grief to be part of my
weeping spheres.

Hanky of this world is so small
Can't wrap up my tears.
I want to end the day with
a day dreams,
but no hopes want to eat
My sympathetic beans,
Cache in my memories
even Flash out,
I feel like this world just

Knockout.
Now The bucket of tears when
Get over filled,
Windy paths pushing me
To become a stilt,
So that you stand in this ocean
with strength,
but jolly butter cuts by the Knife
I can feel there is nothing
For which i have to pray and Rise.
That's why I am saying,
Hanky of the world is small,
Can't wrap up my tears.

3. Wormhole

Looking upon the
Pecies of this home,
Packed in the wall
Of chrome,
You may have shelter
And dome,
But there is nothing
Like web home .
A door with many keys,
A direction where kindness
Winds are covering by the
whole Greed,
A supermarket where you buy
Everything for free,
No reservations of seats,
No charge of homeless freaks,
But they have a long history
The past action of disgrace
And honesty,
They knew all, what you have in
Your wings.

you can hide everything is a myth.
this home will going to turn you
so before entering just check.

• 5 •

4. Lullaby

Into the cloudy land
Silver seats and cotton table
I sit over there in proud.
Gushy people put food
in my plate
Now grumpy weather of
inside have changed.
In the shape of cloud
A land that has been lost
This land has left no resume
To continue
Too many rumours confused
Me about traces of this cloud.
In the shape of cloud
this land of honour,
there are some dreams
That fly with feather,
this cloud belongs to my
mother.

5. The elegant belle

***Here poetess is telling through a story of fondness of men towards a women.**

Vivacious eye
I am watching from
Kelidoscope,
Vivid folklore about her,
Secluded beauty from small
town,
Shadow of this shiny star,
touching my ground.
I am Clinging with the spaces
where she go to draw art,
an acquisition that never left
my door,
a belonging that i live for.
I want to be part of her stillness
Without any gesture
I want to eat caramel tea with her,
I want to tell her
that elegant talk knows,
that she is perfect in her flaws.

6. Chamber of lords

Here Poetess trying to tell her philosphy about the ends of this world
about in the immortal creators and their infinity.

In the chamber of lords
Vanishing covers of secrets,
Lord is a Life without gates
No entry just endless space,
The Tape-recorder have
whining sounds of mercy,
elegant words of percy.
Dwelling places have few days,
But this home of light hold
endless story that we have made.
Drowning in these sea waves
Looking for a boat to cross,
These harsh endless day make you,
come to the land of mercy,
to meet the lords and pray.
But Even in the sea Ends you
Can't find,
the chamber of lords are in
Time.

7. The falling grapes

*here the poetess want to tell that changing life has changed
everything still we have to try to catch the opportunity and treat it
like a last opportunity.

Nothing looks same,
each feeling have different name,
Gaps that we try to fills,
But Now this age gap didn't
gave me, frocks of frills.
Cosmetic we use with base
But wrinkles have their own Space.
Life is getting old.
I found something,
that Change my mind
I try to catch the dropping
Grapes of moment,
Green delicious and full
Of life,
But mysteriously i fall over
My grave,And i realise,
The old version of me was
Full of life,
It was just chasing the lights
But with time love for everything
Have changed,

Everything is just hitting me
To get back in time.
i am trying to catch the last grape.

8. Ability

**here the poetess saying that we can reach things as per our depth
and knowledge but feelings have no factor.*

We can see the things
As far is our vision,
We can think as much as
Far is our mind,
We can greet as much
Humble we are,
We can care as much
Careful we are,
We can taught as much
We have in our selves,
We can show as much
God give to us,
We can flow as much
Fluid we are,
but we can feel more
than we are.

9. Saltbox

In the saltbox of my head,
Inside the drawer of mind,
I have a picture that keep
me remind about golden time.
I am seeking all the memory
in my day dream,
Like trespassing birds in the
garden.
The golden looking floor,
with wrappers of Coffee
that i used morning and night
Colors and paint brushes messed
Over the table and every corner
They roll.
The window bringing light from
The canopy of green climber.
The same old bedsheet and blanket
Unfold,
Dusty valance over the door.
The desk holding the silhouette of
Tree leaves and a notebook
That is full of words.
Now open the cupboard put

ANUSTHA PAL

My on my favoutite dress,
That room was a beautiful mess.

10. Building block

In the cupboard of my mind i have
a house.
With me and my family this house
turn into game.
This house has antique cubic rooms
with desolate genius brains,
There are twenty seven rooms in this house
with four colorful walls but still no colour in lifes,
Top ceiling and basement floor with more
two colours like a small rainbow with little shine,
Like my father, algorithms run this House.
to manage the workflow and to maintain
this colourful house.
If you go and try to fix the ceiling
of top floor and you did it,
so you get smitten colours beautiful
Like rainbow ,
But if you fail you get tangled
into the Colours,
where colours are pell mell in each other.
This algorithm of this house are
complex like iota,

the imaginary problems and
It attached with the real part of life.
Moving from left to right, Up to
bottom,
Every stair havoc you in this Maze,
Only algorithm help you To cross
from this desert to reach the lake,
this house is a complex maze.

11. Shrivels

Poetess here telling about her midnight thoughts.
The bold and hard but never
appreciated.
Innocent and beautiful but
never noticed.
Emotional and humble but
never accepted.
These are the things which
gives me rude awakening.
Whom and why??
These words confronting me and
Craving me to think.
After waiting long hours,
When my energy vanish somewhere
In the dark,
In that nights i am conflicting with
my Psyche,
but getting no point to put light on,
These feelings are murky like a well,
Catching dizzy emotion that i can't spell.
these nights never end and
Take me to these wells.
I stand with Nothing but just
get shrivels.

12. Culprit

here Poetess telling the story of a criminal and how they feel about themselves.

I am slayer hiding in the
walls of grief,
everytime when i kill,
when i take your wheeze,
robbed money with the
help of the knife,
when i am shooting you from my
bullet your shivering body explicate.
People worring and are in
agony.
but i can't murder the memory that
Stuck in my head.
Lying over my bed.
Died,deceased and with
rotten smell.
I rang the mind bells
Roaring and murmering
In a voice that is depress.
but then i knew what i am
today is because of this misery life.
no regrets in my eyes,
but an unwanted person with

an unwanted story,
that nither you nor i m going to
be groove on.

13. Beetles

in this Poetess want to convey that bettle only shine when they fly,
similarly a person when do struggle will shine.

The shiny beetle
When fly, they shine.
Otherwise disappear in the
Darkness of night.
they have to climb on long green
leaves to reach the shiny dew pearl.
they have to walk in the soil and dust.
they have edges to meet, they have
strength to make themselves honourable,
even in clique.
One day you shine in the murky lights
and people get their way through your
burnished path.

14. Little green women

I live in clouds, where life is
full of mist,
lorny and gloomy under the
oak with falling leaves,
I can't see too far,
my life tell me that this is your
life story.
so, one day for a change
i sit over one cloud,
under an oak tree,
i drag my feet and watching
the wind striking
up and down from this sky,
and now clouds dissappear and
there is weird land,
i can see from here what
people are doing,
and when i come to see the
reality of humanity,
i started to fallen in love
with my desolate cloud,

and i thought that,
this emptiness is better
than fake crowd.

15. Billet-doux

here Poetess conveying a love story, when a guy try to own the heart of a girl.

A feather that I left
When I fly,
Furious vicious eyes
When I try,
Flitting balloons in the
Air,
for touching your sky,
Serene love Becoming
serenade
when she looks shy,
looking gorgoues when
for you i wear
a bow tie,
your soft and silky hair
when playing with wind
when they get dry,
i lost my whole heart for
just your one smile.

16. Voice

***here Poetess want to say their what people do in their lives is connected to what they speak and their are voices are indirectly connected to money.**

Listening the whispers

Around me

Looking upon their intensity

And tone

Some voices are remarkable

Like landmark

Some are homeless like refugee

Some having graveyard you

Can't see,

Some are rough like stone

but everyone have a story in

their voice,

some stories are critical and some

full of jolly,

the boundary that separate them is

money.

17. Choice

I m never been before,

I m not horoscope,

I knew I m trying To

become a round Corner,

A never ending edge,

Shoe lashes that are

Not tight when going

To new address,

Shutter of life get Closed

No one for looks over my

The lifestyle and efforts.

I painted my life with colours

that i never loved.

and that's make us what we don't

want to become.

18. The bar

*The poetess telling the scenerio of bars, what are the things she
have seen their*

In these hashy life with cash
having intutions of Lofted trejectory,
watching someone Playing pean loud out
Wear perfect dress with music,
When people create crowd,
flow the music when touch their
ear and beauty remarks,
people spend their everything
with a bottle of bear and ends on
laugh.

19. Falsifier

here Poetess try to tell about liars who are cheating on someone
innocent any how.

Scratch the inner violent socket

Don't put grease on your pocket

There is a lot of dirt on your Shirt,

You need to be honest so don't Flirt.

Your girl Wearing skirt with your locket

She look perfect even in long jacket.

stop being dishonest,

there are long hairs stuck in your pendant

when i stalk it.

do an interspection and absorb it,

otherwise she put you in the life ending

rocket and there is no-one who can stop it.

20. Pashmina

here Poetess is emphasising a story of over pashmina and love,
where she trying to tell the smiliarity in the pashmina and love.

The pashmina shawl
the strings mesmerizing
in the wedding hall
Where my briad is so
Long so I just call,
My wonderful partner to
Hold my dress that fall
On the floor of hall,
and he noticed my pashmina
and said that you have captivated me,
in the strings of yours and
your pashmina,
In every winter pashmina just remind
your words when i wear it,
"everything change but you and your
pashmina never changed".

21. Journey

***here Poetess telling the story by connecting the life journey with a areoplane jounrey.**

The elevator of time
Has taken me to heights,
So I am catching my flight,
The baggage of remaining
Memories is very heavy,
like my suitcase that is over
wait, so i have to pay.
A trip is Memorial that
once i visit,
but after that entire life
is sustained in being fussy
and fidget,
This work of life is as long
As life digits.

22. Loops of dark night

***here poetess want to tell that life has loops of dark night and you
have to out of loop to live a good life.***

The train of dark nights
have Wolfs hiding in twilight,
Jumping over my emotional
Shoe,
I see the lost soul and standing
Without any clue.
This journey turn into a tale
That I am going to tell,
A story on recursion,
A piece of paper with black ink
I try to leave the train
Because wrong trains have infinite
Loops that never end.

23. Blazer

In my blazer
I have a dome that saves
From cold,
Slurpy money have wings
That flows,
Flowers of my kinder garden
ansd smell of marigold,
But my blazer don't know.
In my blazer
i have handkerchief,
that is full of fragrance,
that i gave to my smitten
heart,
Shimmering money that
my mom put in the pocket,
i have used it to buy a new
dress
But my blazer don't know.

24. Five minutes of greed

Five minutes of greed
When you are in your sleep
That greedy part hold an
Uneven mortality
Ease that put you in
Peace,
You feel the whole rest
In the five minutes of greed
May be you get late
Or it should make you feel
The life that you never want
in hills,
But when you end this sleep,
You feel that this greed has
some freed,
you fallen love with this greed.
without this greed
What does life mean??

25. Hazel

***Here the poetess telling about problem and condition of poor
people, how they live their life in difficult situations.***

Hazel in the mid evening

Crossing the roads in the winter cold.

Winds that blows,

Life in this tunnel is

Metaphoric like rust

On the handle of door

Drinking shitty water of Street,

like cowards hides the

Piece of truth,

We are odds on your even

Like a long lasting brook,

I am knitting a peaceful door

And sewing the money that

Flow,

Otherwise I m on street

With a life that is no-more.

26. The dark plot

the way you come down into

my dark plot,

you get clear with me,

clever with me,

others lighten the lamps to write

dark stories about how

scary i can be,

you love the way i bulid

trust,

but still you are shrivering when

see my shadow in the brook,

does you belong to a nobody,

or you want to be somebody?

you don't know how lucid you feel

when i pull your heart out.

the survival of the fitest work

here now,

after that i go beyond to heaven

and you are sadly sitting in your

graveyard with your dead ends.

27. The known

here poetess want to send a message through this poem that sometimes we are too attached and make wrong beliefs and in that times only 'Time' would make you realise to move forward and leave all the others facts behind.

You are my known,
Wishing you at my
Door,
Searching suitable dress
To wear for you,
I am having a face of
smile but with fears,
The insidious girl ask me
Are you sure that he is yours?
In the small town of aisa
Decorating bulbs with siya
Vanishing my life into this world
Just for another amnesia
Cacophony of Maria
Blinking eyes like lights
Packing the tiffin for My
Host who love my food
And it's every bite
The bell rang and I feel
the instincts,

that your feet lying outside
my door,
But when I open the door
There I found just a wind
Who scatter my hair And
A persona so known.
Then i realise how
known become unknown,
this world ends with this
mystery so you have to move
on.

28. Appetite

*here poetess telling about 'Appetite'. The time have their own
illusions which give you appetite for different things.
Appetite that kill you
everytime,
that catch your intention
and make goals within the
given time,
you have taken your brunch
but still there is alot of
hunger in you that lefts
in you,
you ever wish that one
day your appetite end?
like this never-ending starving,
the chronic feeling never end,
whatever you wishing today
if you got,
even than also you don't end.
now you come over another
boat and drifting bows in other side,
one day every appetite end, but
then you also end because
at that time,
you don't left with time.

29. Doors

When does these doors open
Wide?
i am the clover of your tea,
the rising mercury of your thermometer,
the comfort with which you sleep,
the sound that turn into melody,
but when i come to your speech i am
no where.
When does these doors open
Wide?
you make me feel like a stage,
come over and say your words,
then leave,
why you are immersing into
a stone?
i am flames of your life,
did you know how much it take
to become pocket of your
cloths.
When does these doors open
Wide?
So i am standing in the
photoframe in my favourite flannel,
aloof alone but confident enough,

with my gucci bag,
and that make you feel the intensity of your
closed doors that hit to me.
then you run to open the door,
but mist around you tell that you
have lost your gemstone.
so now for meeting once stand in the row.

30. Peace

Sprinkle pureness over
my diminishing soul,
You are living in gaps
of my declining shilloute,
day by day you are taking
one breathe,
You are my well-wisher
or an enemy?
You know as the length of life increase,
then i have to live more,
You know this life is already
have unfinished sea shores,
the umbra inside me travel
over the places in searching the rest,
now she want to sleep in
the crypt to leave all the grief,
now she just want peace.

31. Young

*Here the poetess is telling about the youngesters and how some good people mostly parents come in their life and raise them,give them direction.

In every lost mind, there are lost

spaces,

Where everything is secondary

and adjustable for the new age.

Holding hands in the colourful

dresses blue,yellow orange and

grey.

No worry if pockets are empty

cause there are several other

ways.

there is always some angels

behind your back,

who help you in your growing days,

who guide you to find your way.

they hold your hand until the last

stage.

32. Intertia

***here Poetess want to tell that everything have their own value and purpose.**

Inertia of this lifestyle Is high,
Giving jerks to the bus of life,
I am loathed weapon that
you have choose,
but when foe are near
i will shoot.
A garage having few Tools,
but when you park your car
i will repair you in a few.
A dim light that is useless for you,
but when you in the dark
this light become your angel,
So the interia of life tell you are
important even if you are futile.
just calm and live for a while.

Thankyou so much to all my readers :)